On Life and Love

On Life and Love

M. Christine Stephens

Xulon Press
2301 Lucien Way #415
Maitland, FL 32751
407.339.4217
www.xulonpress.com

© 2017 by M. Christine Stephens

All rights reserved solely by the author. The author guarantees all contents are original and do not infringe upon the legal rights of any other person or work. No part of this book may be reproduced in any form without the permission of the author. The views expressed in this book are not necessarily those of the publisher.

Scripture quotations taken from the Holy Bible, New International Version of the Quest Study Bible revised (NIV). Copyright © 1994, 2003 by Zondervan Publishers. Used by permission. All rights reserved

This book contains approximately 15,700 words.

10705 Sunrise Terrace Dr. Orlando, FL 32825
Cell 727-906-2710
Email : christine5678@gmail.com

Printed in the United States of America.

ISBN-13: 9781545615713

Acknowledgment

Thank you for letting me write this book, and thank you for reading it. Thank you God for giving me the time and the provision to write. Thank you Dale for buying me the computer to type it on, and all the help you've given to me. Thank you to the publisher that proofread it, corrected my errors, believed that this would be a good book, and took a chance on this unknown author. I hope you like it.

The title of this book is On Life and Love; it is a collection of twenty-two very short stories that touch on many different circumstances of life, and God's word of truth in each of those. My intended readers and audiences are pastors, their congregations, the saved and the unsaved: those that love the Lord and those who have yet to enjoy a close relationship with Him. This book could be a tool to ministry in a church service, a Bible study, in a youth group ministry, or as a life story source, from which a minister could draw a teaching, sermon or illustration. Many, many times that is the very way Jesus taught, in stories and parables that caused the hearer to think. I feel I am qualified to write this not because of who I am, but because of who Christ is. Jesus did not call the qualified; He qualified the called. He used a man with impaired speech to tell a Pharaoh in Egypt to let God's people go. He used a boy to kill a giant, a fishermen to become a fisher of men, and a young village girl to give birth to the King of kings and the Lord of lords. We are only ever qualified to write for the Lord, or to serve Him or know Him or love Him, not because we meet qualifications, but because

M. Christine Stephens

He loves us. Because He wants to use us for His kingdom, we belong to Him and we have sonship. He paid a debt we could not pay to allow us not only salvation, but to have a relationship with God. This is the only, yet the greatest, qualification I can present to you. We are His voice here on earth; who, if not those of us who love Him, are qualified? I have been a physical therapy caregiver most of my adult life. I worked in home health care, and I have worked in hospitals for years. I was a police officer, I am a mother, daughter, sister, grandmother, wife, and friend. I have been at deathbeds, crime scenes, birthing centers, ghettos, mansions, and jail houses: and in all of these, I have seen God's grace. There is nowhere God's Holy Spirit cannot go. I taught at Faith Community Church, a non-denominational church in Pinellas County, Florida, in the Sonlight youth ministry, and taught God's Word at the juvenile detention center in Pinellas County, Florida as an outreach of our church. These short stories deal with the stuff of everyday life, and with God's grace, mercy, deliverance, forgiveness, redemption, and everlasting love in all of them. I hope this book will be of use to pastors, ministers, and youth group leaders everywhere. I hope you give this unknown author a chance, and I hope you like the book. I love the times in church when a story was read from the pulpit, and a moral lesson and a truth from God's Word was imparted to the hearer in that way. When I think about it, that was often the very way Jesus taught, in stories and parables that imparted a truth to the hearer. Thanks a million for considering this book.

Christine

November 12, 2016

This book, entitled **On Life and Love**, is designed to reach the unsaved, the unchurched, and the people who would not read about God. When I did not love God, I would not ever have read a book that talked openly about salvation, redemption, healing, mercy, grace, or forgiveness. I am more thankful now than I could ever say for all of those things, but there was a day that if I picked up a book and read about those things, I would not continue to read it. I love every Max Lucado, Joyce Meyers, and Andrew Wommack that write books to teach and encourage those of us who know and love God. They are precious, and they helped me in a thousand ways, but this is not that kind of book. This book was written to entertain the ungodly, and when they least expect it and before they know it, they have been courted with God's Word. I know the words I write will not change people's hearts; the Holy Spirit is the only heart-changer. My hope is to hold their attention long enough with a secular story that's easy to read, and keep them reading until God's Word is delivered at

M. Christine Stephens

the end; in small doses that they can absorb. We know that never comes back void. I know how hard it is for unknown authors to ever get their work published. I am asking you to give this book a chance. Thanks a million.

Thank you for your consideration.

Sincerely,
Mary Christine Stephens

Chapters:

1. Cockroach Peanut Butter 1
2. Judge Lee and the Three Gold Diggers. 5
3. An Only Child 9
4. Brilliant Lanny 12
5. Divine Appointment 16
6. Grandma Grace 18
7. Honoring Grandma's Memory 21
8. Like the Wind 24
9. Mission Statement 26
10. Tell Me About a Boy 31
11. That Just Doesn't Seem Fair 34
12. The French Fry Method 37
13. The Real Deal 40
14. The Spider-Webbed Sewer Machine 43
15. They Are All Hypocrites 47
16. Changing Grace 49
17. Miss June and the Norfolk Pine 54
18. Mr. Garwood and Woody 58
19. Saltwater Fish 63
20. Final Payment for Kaitlin 65
21. The Spirit Realm 70
22. The Jigsaw Puzzle 72

Cockroach Peanut Butter

I did home health care for a lot of years; I went into people's homes and did their physical therapy with them there. I have been in million-dollar homes and homes in the ghetto. I have been in mansions on the water and, an hour later, in the public housing projects. You see a lot: the good, the bad, and the ugly. Let me tell you about Mr. Rasey. I could smell the stench of his tiny apartment through the screen door. I knocked, but he could not get out of bed to let me in. Just come in, he barked, so I did. Everything about Mr. Rasey and that apartment was appalling; it was filthy throughout. The floor was slippery from urine. There was no food in the cupboards or fridge. The garbage can overflowed onto the floor and was caked with the remnants of food gone by. I just kept thinking, how can anyone live like this. Mr. Rasey's fingernails were long and caked beneath with I don't know what. His hair was long and greasy, and the stench of body odor hung in the room so that it was offensive to breath. It took me a few minutes to take a visual inventory and process it all. Beside his bed was an open jar of peanut butter, with a knife stuck in it, and three cockroaches. Is this what you have been eating? Yep, he said, for a while. I made a resolve to do what I could for him on that visit and get him help. When I returned to my office, I told the other therapist there about Mr. Rasey's wretched condition. Does he have any family? They told me he had a son up north somewhere, so I got that number from the old man's chart and called his son. The call went just like this: Hello. My name is Christine. I am a home health therapist for your father here in Florida; is this his son? I'm calling to let you know about the condition of your father here. I know you don't live close by so I'm not sure if you know, but it is bad and I need to talk to you about it. The son's response was slow. He told me he was working now and could not talk, but he would call me back tonight when we could discuss it. I gave him my cell phone number, and told him I would wait for his call. That night came and went, and he did not call me. I called again the following night, but young Mr. Rasey did not answer. I called again the next morning, and he did answer. There was irritation in his voice, but he let me tell him that I was concerned for his father's welfare. I told him about the filth, the lack of food and personal hygiene, the stench, and the apparent helplessness of his dad. Then I told him about the cockroach peanut butter. He listened for a moment, and then he couldn't contain his irritation with me any longer. This was his reply: Look lady, I am at work, and I am busy. I have to earn a living. My father was a brutal and callous man, and now he is helpless and old, kind of like a toothless lion. We have been disconnected for a very long time, for as long as I can remember. I don't care about him, and he has never cared about me. I don't care if he eats cockroach peanut butter. He is getting what he has coming to him. When I was a little boy, he kicked me across the street if I didn't move fast enough. He didn't care if I had socks, he never knew or cared what grade I was in, and I was not allowed to play football in high school because the shoes and the mouthpiece cost money, but he always had money for liquor; lots and lots of liquor. He didn't care about me, so now I don't care about him. I am trying to work today, so I don't have time to talk to you. I live up north; I am not in Florida enough to do anything for him, or help him in any way. I have a family and kids now, and that's who I take care of. I cannot interrupt my work, or my life, to worry about him. Isn't there some social agency you can call for him? I don't mean to be rude to you, but you keep calling me, so I'm just asking you to stop. I have to go back to work; and with that, he hung up. I wanted to talk to him longer. I wanted to talk to him about forgiveness, about giving people second chances, about a lot of things, but I did not get the chance. I called a social service agency for his father, because they have options that will help him.

That which a man sows shall he also reap.

> Don't be deceived. God can not be mocked. A
> man reaps what he sows. Galations 6:7 NIV

Judge Lee and the Three Gold Diggers

I met Judge Lee when he was very old, living in a nursing home. I worked there as a therapist in the physical therapy gym, and every day, the rehab tech would wheel him down to the gym for therapy. The good judge was crippled and bent, riddled with arthritis and Parkinson's disease. He shook uncontrollably, his shirt was always wet with drool, and although his mind was crystal clear, it was trapped in a body that would never again do his bidding. Judge Lee was once a prominent figure in the community. He had a reputation for fairness and mercy, tempered with years of experience and good old common sense. I liked him. What I could do for him physically was very limited, but we talked a lot about a lot of things, and this seemed to be the right therapy for Judge Lee, and what helped him most; so that's what I did. As we became friends, I asked him, in a kind of friendly and casual way, if he had any regrets in life. He told me that it's not so much that he regrets things he did, but rather things he didn't do. That was profound

M. Christine Stephens

and I never forgot it. I stopped in his room from time to time, if I had a minute, just to say hello; and almost always, there was a young, beautiful women at his bedside. They played cards, ate cookies, watched old movies, and talked. I just assumed she was a daughter, granddaughter; I wasn't sure. I never asked and he never told me. Judge Lee had two sons, and, on rare occasions, I would see them visiting, too. One morning, before the therapy gym was open, there was a knock at the door. The work day was soon to start, so I unlocked it. It was Judge Lee's sons; they asked me not to let that women who was always with their father in the therapy gym when Dad was having therapy. I sensed they did not like her and resented the time she spent with their father. As we spoke, I could see that it was more and more difficult for them to hide their contempt for her. The younger son finally blurted out, "She is a gold digger. She is out to marry our father, and he is a wealthy man. She does not love him at all; what does this young, pretty blonde want with my father, except for his money? I just listened and let them vent; and when they were finished, I explained that if Judge Lee wanted her there, then she may accompany him; that there is no rule against that, and because the judge was of sound mind, I would honor whatever he wanted. The sons were not happy to hear what I told them, and what I think they already knew. They left, and I began my work day. Shortly thereafter, the rehab tech

On Life and Love

wheels Judge Lee in, like he has many other days. Judge Lee seemed withdrawn today; I just said hello and let him talk first. Did my sons come and talk to you this morning? he asked. I told him yes they did. They do not like my lady friend. They object to our relationship, and they fear she is using me to get something from me. They are aware of my intention to marry her, and they have warned me against it. They call her a gold digger. Judge Lee looked at his wet shirt and apologized for his appearance. No worries, I told him. He told me she comes every day to change his shirt, and she brings cookies. They watch old movies and play poker, and her visits are the highlight of his world. Do you think she is using me? I told him I could not answer that, because I don't know her. I strongly suspected she was, but could not bring myself to say that. I think, deep down, Judge Lee thought so, too, but I believe that he wanted to believe that she loved him. I would never have said otherwise. Do you know what I think? I think my sons are gold diggers; I sent both of those men to law school, and I set both up in law practices. I gave both down payments on beautiful homes; I have helped their children through college, bought them their first cars, and have just generally given to all of them abundantly. I don't have much time left. I have accrued some wealth along the way, and these two sons want to be certain that they get it; and they are afraid that if I marry her, they won't. Yet, she is the one that is here with me every day. They are busy and absent, and off in life to seek their fortunes. Without Maria's company, I would be here mostly alone, and I would die mostly alone. I don't think my sons have ever stopped to consider that. I don't feel like I owe them anything more. If Maria is a comfort to me, and she is, then why could they not be happy for me? Why don't they love me enough to be happy that I don't eat cookies and watch old movies alone? They say Maria's company is just something that I buy. If a man can afford to buy something he wants, why shouldn't he? My wife died of cancer many years ago, and since then the loneliness has been unbearable. For me, I thought, I would not want to purchase any one's love, companionship, or allegiance: but I am not old and crippled and alone, so I will not judge that. His point was well taken. I wasn't sure how to answer him. I wasn't sure what hurt him more: the realization of his adult sons' greed, or the fact that as much as he wanted Maria there, he, deep down, realized why she was.

Honor thy father and mother, so that your days on this earth will be long.

> Honor thy father and mother, so that you may live long in the land that your Lord your God is giving you. Exodus 20:12 NIV

An Only Child

I had three brothers and three sisters, so there were seven of us all together. I love having a lot of siblings. We are each other's friends: we hang out together, we talk a lot, and we have a built-in circle of friends to do things with so, overall, it's pretty great. When I was younger though, I sometimes wished I was an only child. My best friend in school was an only child. Her parents doted on her, and she pretty much got everything and anything she wanted. Their whole world seemed to be about only her, and everything she had was new and nice and the best of the best, and a lot of it. I was always a little bit jealous of that. My family didn't have much money. My father worked hard and he provided for his family, but there were nine of us to provide for; and not much left for the nicer things in life. I was the third-born girl; I had two older sisters. Sometimes, I wore their secondhand clothes. I remember going to her house to hang out. Her bedroom was beautiful: the furniture was classy; the bedding matched the curtains and the rugs. Her clothes were awesome: always new shoes, jewelry, make-up, money anytime she asked for it, and even when she didn't, a new car in high school, and college money already tucked away for her. I loved my brothers and sisters with all my heart, but there were many times I wished I was an only child, and I told her that. She told me exactly the opposite was true for her, and she would trade places with me in a minute. For me, she seemed so loved, so pampered, so cared for, and so special. I always felt like one of many, lost in the shuffle, and had a take-whatever-you-get-kind of deal in life. It's not that my parents didn't try, because they did: it's that sometimes there were too many to care for, too much to take care of, not-enough-to-go-around kind of life. Now that I am grown, I see that a lot of good things came out of that. We were not spoiled; we knew that you had to work hard for whatever you got; you learned that no one was going to cater to you in life; and no one owed you anything. All of this is true, and a great life lesson, and it made you strong and independent. You were not a crybaby, and you did not wait for anyone to hand you anything; and it helped me navigate life correctly in many ways. Looking back, I am thankful for that. There were times in my adult life, though, and they were times of sadness and hardship that I wanted to be God's only child. I knew, realistically, that I was not and never would be God's only child: but in some of the

On Life and Love

hardest times, I would ask God if just for now, or just for a little while, I could be His only child. He let me, and I love Him for that. People ask me now if I am religious, but I tell them, very truly, I am not. For me, it's not about religion; it's about a love.

I love you with an everlasting love.

> The Lord has appeared to s in the past, saying
> " I love you with an everlasting love, I have drawn you with my unfailing kindness.
>
> Jeremiah 31:3 NIV

Brilliant Lanny

The things someone tells you when you are young affect you, sometimes for a lifetime. When you are young, you are impressionable; your personality can be molded. The words that are spoken to you have power over you. You are not yet old enough or wise enough to discern whether they are true or correct. You just hear them and take them to heart. My first real boyfriend in high school was a guy named Lanny. He played the guitar like Jimi Hendricks, played the keyboard, and fixed all his buddies' old, beater cars: because that was back in the day before computers were in cars, and you could fix them yourself. He sold marijuana to anyone in high school that wanted to buy it; he was the underground entrepreneur, and he ran it like the business it was to him. He fixed our eight-track tape players, fixed our radios, and calculated the times that were more likely to be safe to smoke weed in our hangout spot by the Allegheny River; because his cousin was a cop, and told him who usually patrols there and how often. He knew a hundred card tricks and magic tricks, and could

On Life and Love

remember a series of numbers, all kinds of numbers. He remembered everyone's phone numbers and addresses, and memorized every single detail on a one, five, ten, twenty and fifty-dollar bill. He had a memory like a steel trap, was smart as a whip, and ran numbers with his older brother in the underground Italian neighborhood where he lived. He organized football polls and knew more card games than I ever heard of, but he never did well in school. He flunked English three times, struggled in math, and when he went to school, at all, was the class clown. He had to repeat two different grades two separate times, so he was two years older than most of us in high school. I can remember back then thinking how smart he was in so many things, so why was he so bad at school? Why was it that he could barely get through school? I could tell he was embarrassed about that, so I never really talked about it with him too much, but one day he said something to me that answered that question. He said his mother always told him he was as dumb as a jackass; she always told him that he was pretty much worthless, and was never going to amount to much. He told me that he really believed that, and he was afraid to go to school for as long as he could ever remember. He said when he started the first grade, he knew he would have to be smart to remember letters and numbers, to read and write, and do all the things the other kids were learning to do, but he thought he was as dumb as a jackass so he tuned out. I was afraid, he told me. I was always afraid. I knew everyone else could learn all that because they were smart, or at least okay. I knew I was dumb, and I probably couldn't do it, so I didn't try. I just kind of quit before I started. I remember thinking about how sad that was. Lanny was one of the smartest guys I ever knew. He was friends with everyone: the nerds, the geeks, the jocks, the hippies, and the bookworms. Everyone loved Lanny. He was sharp and witty, could connect with everyone and anyone, and navigated things most people twice his age could not. Even though the businesses he ran were clandestine and dirty, he ran them. He juggled a dozen things in his mind, and could talk to anyone about anything. He was warm and friendly, and if there was a problem, he had a solution. He worked by night, went to school by day, fixed cars, played instruments, and was the underground businessman of more than one dirty venture. He had the energy of ten guys, the savvy of a politician, and a hundred other qualities that would have taken him very far, and led him to tremendous success in the legitimate world, except for one nagging problem. Somebody that Lanny loved, trusted, and looked up to a long time ago told him he was stupid, and he believed it. Somebody whose job it was to encourage him and lift him up told him he was worthless, and he bought into that. More than anything else,

On Life and Love

this is what I learned from knowing Lanny; be careful what you say to people. Be especially careful about what you say to your kids, because whether you are right or wrong, they will believe you; and that just might make them or break them.

Words have the power of life or death.

> The tongue has the power of life and death, and those who love it will eat its fruits.
>
> Proverbs 18:21 NIV

Divine Appointment

I took my kids to Gulfport Beach when they were little. There was a playground; they loved to dig in the sand and swim. It was Monday morning; the beach was quiet and empty, except for two ladies sitting at a picnic table playing cards. I had the two-year-old on my hip, and the six-year-old swam near my feet. We kicked at waves and looked for seashells. Out of nowhere, a little girl came up from the water and was running towards the beach. She was sobbing, saying something like "She tried to drown me, " between sobs, or that's what it sounded like. Who tried to drown you? I asked. No reply. She just ran towards the ladies playing cards. I looked around, but no one was there. I wasn't sure I even heard her right. Off a few yards, I saw something light submerged under the water. It looked like an old milk jug, or maybe a garbage bag; it was under, and I couldn't make it out. I didn't think much about it at first, then my curiosity got to me. I walked over to it, baby still in my arms and on my hip, to pick it up. I reached down into the water to retrieve it and, to my horror, it was a cold and, apparently, lifeless little girl. I had one free arm to pick her up; she didn't cry or struggle. She was limp and seemed to be lifeless. I ran through the waves and to the beach, and laid her in the sand. I screamed to the ladies at the picnic table, somebody help me. The lady ran toward her screaming, " Oh my God." I pressed on her tiny chest, and water spurted out. She vomited. She sucked in a breath, and then a faint cough and gag: a tiny cry, then a full-blown sob. Thank God, the lady playing cards said. I was watching them; I really was. I was only distracted for a minute. The little girl was okay, but it made me think about divine appointments. Sometimes we are exactly where we need to be exactly when we need to be there. I remind myself of that when I am running late and frustrated, or when something interrupts my plans. Next time that happens to you, just remember; maybe it was supposed to.

He will give His angels charge over you.

> For He command His angels concerning you to
> guard you in all of your ways. Psalms 91:11 NIV

Grandma Grace

I loved my grandma; we called her Grandma Grace. She had a house in the alley in what is now a run-down, dilapidated neighborhood in a place called Wilkinsburg in Pennsylvania. She died a long time ago, but I have some of the best childhood memories of my life at Grandma Grace's house. There was a spinning platter filled with every kind of candy you could imagine. There were candy necklaces, candy rings, and licorice whips: Black Cows, Sugar Babies, Necco® wafers and Ju Ju Beads. There were Mary Janes, Razzles and Jawbreakers. No one ever yelled at you at Grandma's house, and then there was the store down the street; it was called John's Bargain Store. It had punching bags, stuffed animals on sticks and strings, cheap jewelry, and jewelry boxes; the kind that played music and the ballerina danced when you opened the lid. We got to eat unlimited amounts of sugar, and no one worried about it. There was Hershey kisses, and you could have as many of them as you wanted, all day long. My grandma was loud and rowdy, never worried about the political correctness of anything, and had a straw hat with a rubber cow on top that she wore on family reunions. It had a wire connected to a battery pack that you held in your hand, and you could light up the cows' eyes. She went to an old Catholic church, and when she died, they had her funeral there. The priest did his best to honor her in his eulogy. He told people how she helped in the church, how she volunteered, and how much everyone will miss her, and then he did something that surprised me back in that day. He asked her family to finish the eulogy; you see, he knew about her, but we knew her. He wouldn't have known about the cow hat and the Jawbreakers. He never saw her rowdy side, because he only saw her in church. It made me think of how I knew about God way back, and how I know Him now. As a child, I knew God was up there somewhere. I thought He was okay with me if I did good things, and mad at me when I didn't. He was kind of scary, and there were a lot of things you had to keep from Him because He just wouldn't understand; or even if He did, He wouldn't like it. That's what I knew, or thought I knew, about God back then. Now I know He is more like my grandma than I thought. He loves me just because He does. I don't have to be good enough or right enough; I don't have to do and say all the right things at all the right times. He was more like this, and I finally got it when I became a parent, too.

M. Christine Stephens

God is a parent. When I brought my baby home, I loved her just because I loved her. She was never required to earn my love. She threw up constantly, cried all night, dirtied a thousand diapers, made a thousand messes, cost me thousands of dollars, so everything she did was not conducive to earning love. Here's the good news: she never had to earn my love. I loved her no matter what she did or did not do. My love for her was never based on her behavior, and neither is God's love for us. Sure, he wants us to do good, but it is not why He loves us. His love is not based on this or that, or if I do more of this and less of that. Aren't we lucky?

You are the apple of my eye. I love you with an everlasting love.

> For this is what the Lord Almighty says; "After the Glorious One has sent me against the nations that have plundered you for whoever touches you touches the apple of my eye.
>
> Zachariah 2:8

Honoring Grandma's Memory

I worked in a rehab facility with a therapist named Calli. She had a twin sister that she has not spoken to in six years. They each had a little boy, one four months older than the other; kind of like a second generation, almost second set of almost twins. Calli told me she never met her sister's little boy. The boys have never played together, and did not know each other. What in the world, I wondered, could have happened to make these sisters so angry? What could be so bad that these semi-sibling cousins could not run, ride bikes, swim and play together? Calli told me she looked on her sister's Facebook, and although they were not friends and did not correspond, she could see pictures. She talked about her sister a lot, so I knew her sister was on her mind nearly every day; and I just blurted out what I thought a thousand times, What happened to make you two so mad? Calli told me that when their grandmother passed away, her sister took Grandma's wedding ring. Calli told me the ring was very expensive, but went on to say that the money was not the point. The issue, she said, was that she was born ten minutes before her sister and in her family, the oldest granddaughter got the maternal grandmother's wedding ring. That's the way it was in her family, so that ring should have rightfully went to her, but her sister took it. It's not about the worth of the ring, said Calli; it's that it should be mine, and I wanted it to honor my grandmother's memory. I thought about that. Don't you think it would honor your grandmother's memory more if you love and forgave her granddaughter? Wouldn't it be a greater honor to her memory to know and love your nephew, and let those two little boys be cousins? Like Dr. Phil always says, " This relationship needs a hero." Be a hero today Calli; go call your sister. It's just a piece of jewelry. Forgive her, and let it go. Have Christmas dinner this year with your sister and her family. It will be a blessing to your mom, and thus an honor to her mom, your grandma. Then you will truly and, in deed, honor your grandmother's memory. Forgiveness frees the forgiver, not the forgiven. I told Calli about a talk show I watched years ago. Loni Anderson, the beautiful ex-wife of Burt Reynolds, was being interviewed. She was asked if she forgave Burt, and visa versa, for whatever destroyed their marriage. She assured the audience that she did. I did forgive him, because bitterness makes you ugly, and I don't want to be ugly. That was profound, and I never forgot it. It is one reason, among

On Life and Love

many, to forgive. Forgiveness is conditional; we don't get it unless we give it, and, at some point, we all need it and don't deserve it. Forgive one another, as God has forgiven you.

> Be kind and compassionate to one another, forgiving each other, just as in Christ god forgave you. Ephesians 4:32

Like the Wind

What is a Holy Ghost? I remember when I was a kid, I heard that in Catholic school all the time, but no one ever really told me what it was. I kind of knew who God was, and I kind of knew who Jesus was, or at least that He died on a cross, because I saw pictures of that, but a Holy Ghost? All I knew about ghosts were that they were white, like a bedsheet, and they lived in haunted houses, but a holy one? I could never connect it all in my mind, so I just forgot about it for a long time. Kids are funny like that. They see a picture, the image in their minds is set, and that is what they think. When I got older, I met an old black preacher man at my friend's house. He had a raspy voice like Louis Armstrong, and he was talking about the Holy Ghost. What is that, I finally asked. I never really got the drift of that one; is it like a ghost that haunts people at night? Let me see, he said. How do I explain the Holy Ghost? He is like the wind. You can't see Him, but He is real. You see evidence of it when a tree limb moves, or when your hair blows around on a windy day. You can't see the wind, but you feel it

On Life and Love

on your face and you know it's there. Sometimes it moves slow and gentle, and it blows a piece of paper off the picnic table. Sometimes it is fast and strong, and it can blow down a building. Over time, it can cut through stone, and it has the power to change the course and direction of a tiny kayak or the largest ship. There is no power that can stand against it. The wind changes things: it can move water; it can move a cloud to let the sun shine down. No one can control it. You cannot stop it or start it. You can't catch it or channel it, or tell it how fast or slow to go. You can react or respond to it, but that's all. Sometimes the wind is cold, and it makes you shudder. Sometimes it is warm like the summertime. You can't run away from it because it is all around you. It's the character of God that moves us, directs us, deals with us, and calls to us. It is the wind that blows dead leaves off the trees in the autumn, and dead branches from a tree in the spring, so new branches can grow. We feel it, because it is there and because it is real. The wind touches you. There's more I could say, but that's enough for you to think about now.

And the Spirit of God moved across the water.

> Now the earth was formless and empty, darkness was over the surface of the deep, and the spirit of god was hovering over the waters.
>
> Genesis 1:2

Mission Statement

In high school, I could have been voted the most likely to hate corporate America. Okay, maybe I shouldn't say hate. Lots of corporations are good, and they deserve to make fair and reasonable profits. I never liked business, and when someone tells me he/she majored in management, or a business-related field in college, I still shudder, but that's just me. Don't hate me: maybe I just hate it because I would never be any good at it; or because I don't always entirely trust it all of the time. Sure, there are lots of good and legitimate businesses that serve and help a lot of good people in very honorable ways, and I know that. I also knew that there were some that did not, so I was always skeptical; but I always held jobs and worked, and that involves, on some direct or indirect way, being in the business world. There was this question employers always used to ask me on job interviews: Where do you see yourself in five years from now? Where do you want to be? I'll admit I never really knew how to answer that. What did they want me to say? Did they want me to say I wanted to gouge my way to the top, work twelve hours a day, and never take off a business shirt? I was sure I didn't want to do all those things, but could I say that? Here's what I wanted to say: I want to kayak on Thursdays. I like the smell of wet earth and water. I want to do better at remembering people's birthdays, or bringing my neighbor a casserole when she's sick. I wanted to write a book. I wanted to work less and play with my kids more. I don't want to work overtime. I wanted to be the one that leaves when my shift is finished, because I had things in my life that were more important to me than work and making money. Then they always had what they called a company motto, or a mission statement, and it always went something like this: We care about our patients, customers first. We strive to please them and put their needs before ours, with compassion and caring, or some variation of that. I wanted to believe them. It sounded great and noble, and if that was true, that was a great way to run a business; but a lot of times, it was not. I learned that sometimes business is way less about that, and way more about the bottom line. I guess they shouldn't have to apologize or make excuses for that; after all, isn't that what business is really about, making money? Every business has to make money, or it will not survive, not be able to pay anyone, and employees and their families will suffer; so I get all that, I really do. Physical therapy was my profession, my line of work. Sometimes, I was able to help some people and make tremendous differences in their lives and sometimes, for a variety of reasons, I was not. There were lots of times people just didn't want to. They were old and tired, or they were getting along fine just like they were: they were not going to change a thing they did and they told me so; and what they wanted most was to be left alone. I would try to encourage them to try and to work with me, but in the end, I wanted to be able to respect their wishes and accept the fact that they did not want my services. Sometimes, people were making tremendous strides in therapy. They came to the gym and loved it. They were motivated. They worked hard, were getting better, they followed through on what you asked them to do, and their lives were better, easier, safer, or less painful because of that. They were a therapist dream to work with. Here's my point in telling you all of that: when I was younger and more naive, I thought the course of therapy should be based on that; on what did or did not benefit them most, but more often than not, that was not true. The course, frequency, and duration of therapy were based on what the paying source was: who had insurance, and who did not; how long Medicare would pay for something, or when that maximum number was reached. We were taught what to write and not to write in a chart, so we would not get a Medicare claim denied. We were taught to push people who did

On Life and Love

not want to work with us, because that was money we could not afford to lose. We were told to present it as if the company cared about their progress, but that was more false than true. I grew to hate all of those things. I was dealing with people's lives, but was forced to do it as if they were only resources of revenue. I never liked money. I know we need it to survive in this world. I always earned money, spent money, paid bills, bought houses and cars, and did all the things we all have to do: but, deep down, I always hated what money, or more accurately the love of money, caused people to do. It changed people; it made them greedy and aggressive, and willing to step on whoever they had to get it. I saw that for people who love money, they never could get enough. They are not happy with having enough to meet their needs; they are always driven to have more. They become a bottomless pit of unsatisfied greed. They talk about money continually. They think about it all the time, and every situation they encounter in life, they see it through the filter of money. Every decision they ever make revolves around money, and whoever gets hurt in the process becomes collateral damage. It is gross and evil and brutal, and against everything I think. I cannot devote myself to that cause. I cannot give allegiance to that mentality, and probably the reason I will never have lots of it. I think most of corruption, deceit, and abuse in this world is either directly, or indirectly, related to the

M. Christine Stephens

love of money. If you want to uncover most of what is dark in the world, just follow the money trail.

> For the love of money is the root of all kind of evil. Some people, eager for money, have wandered form the faith and pierced themselves with many griefs. I Ttimothy 6:10

Tell Me About a Boy

My grandson and I play this game. He starts by saying this, "Tell me about a boy." I can then tell him anything I want. I can tell him any story I want about any boy. He wants it to be fast-moving, great to listen to, full of action and drama, or adventure or mishap: but it better be a good one, or he will lose interest fast. It does not have to be a good story with a good moral or a happy ending. It can be about a bad boy who did something wrong and got caught up in it. It can have a bad ending, or even a sad or scary or terrible ending. Being a grandmother, I do try to make it a story with a good moral life lesson, but he is more interested in the story, not the lesson. We love a juicy story; it is hard not to get caught up in that. It is hard not to want to know who did this or that; how or why or when they did it; who they did it with or to; and what happened to them because of that. We like it when it's juicy. Why are we like that? Even when we know it's wrong to gossip, we find it hard to resist. Even though we would not like anyone to say anything about us, if we were not there to give our sides of the story, we want to hear it anyway. What creepy thing in our nature likes that? Maybe it can make us feel better about ourselves. Maybe we get to say something like this to ourselves. Wow, I might have done some bad things, but I never would have done that! Maybe it lets us think look into the lives of other people, to see their hardships, their weaknesses and struggles, their fears and failures, and faults. Sometimes, if we are honest, we are more interested in the bad things people do then in the good ones. Maybe it comforts us to know we are not the only ones that do bad things, or that our lives, as hard as they can be, are still not that bad. The older I get, I try not to engage in gossip. I admit that sometimes I have to fight hard against that, and I'm getting better and better about that as time goes on. It's not so much that I said slanderous and bad things about other people. I was pretty good at not doing that. The bigger problem for me was that for some reason, I just wanted to hear it. I'm learning to say, "You know what, that person is not here right now to defend him/herself, or tell his/her side of the story." I'm getting better at saying, "I don't need to know that," or "If that was said in confidence to you, just don't tell me." I am getting better at remembering this. Those who gossip to you will gossip about you. I'm learning to have a good motive when I say to someone, "Tell me about a boy."

On Life and Love

A gossip betrays a confidence, but a trustworthy person keeps a secret. Proverbs 11:13

That Just Doesn't Seem Fair

Kids have a keen sense of justice; they want fairness in life. They watch when you pour their brother a glass of chocolate milk; the glass that is right beside the one you're pouring for them. They want it to be equal. They will get mad if their brother's glass is filled even a tiny bit fuller than theirs. They pay attention to who gets what. They eye up the pile of Christmas gifts under the tree compared to their own. They calculate who got what from who, and how it compares to what they got. I guess, if we will all be honest, we all do that. Why did someone else get something in life that we didn't get? What made them so special? When we grow up, it becomes less about chocolate milk and more about who was lucky enough to be born rich, or beautiful, or smart, or have a better advantage in life. We try to be happy for other people when really good things in life happen for them; and we know that we should, but somewhere deep down inside, we can't help but think, why did that happen for them and not for me? What about me? When is it going to be

On Life and Love

my turn to win? It's human nature to think those things, and we all do it sometimes. We all think things like, sure, I could be in a better position in life, too, if I had the luck that other person had. If I was born thinner or richer, smarter or luckier, healthier or stronger, bigger or smaller, at another time or place, into another family or circumstance: well, you get the drift. That list could go on and on and on. When my kids were little, if one got something the other one didn't, the first thing he/she said was, hey, that's not fair. They figured out in life, very early on, that life did not seem fair. When I was a kid, there were times in my life when I would say to my grandma, "Life is not fair". Then she would say, "And don't you forget that." Who decides what fair is? Who decides who is going to be able to run faster, jump higher, make more money, get more attention, get more of what they want, be more talented, or be able to study less and get better grades? Who decides who gets the breaks in life? Who gets the faster car, the prettier girlfriends, and the bigger cookie? Again, I could go on and on and on, but I think you get the drift of what I'm saying here. I guess I said all of that to say this. There are things in life we will never be able to figure out and understand. We can get mad, we can get sad, and we can get bitter, or we can accept it and be okay with it. We can recognize that we all have different gifts in life, but we all have some gifts. We can help our kids learn that;

we can be careful to always treat them fairly and equally. We can always let them know we don't have a favorite, and we love them each the same. We can teach them not to compare themselves to other people, but to always do the very best with what God gave them. We can teach them that there are some things in life that we will never completely understand, but not to get too bogged down with that. We can teach them that the only thing they can control, change, and correct is themselves and their own behavior. We can teach them that the only life they will be accountable for is their own. That knowledge will help them be less envious and less judgmental, because there will always be people who seem to be either better or worse off than they are. We can teach them that in this life, sometimes we don't know the reasons for things. We don't always get to know the answer to everything.

The most High is Sovereign.

> "The decision is announced by messengers, the Holy ones declare the verdict, so that the living may know that the Most High is sovereign over all kingdoms on earth and gives them to anyone He wishes and sets over them the lowliest of people. Daniel 4:17

The French Fry Method

My friend Kelly and I talk a lot about our childhoods: the things we thought were good and right, the things we thought were bad and wrong, the funny things, the sad things, and the hard things. We talked about relationships between sisters and just about everything else women talk about. We talked about work and men and life and love. I'm sure all friends do that. I forget what led up to this, but she told me a story that I will always remember. I call it the French fry method. She told me that her sister and her both loved French fries; I guess most kids do. Her mother hardly ever made French fries, mostly because they were a hassle to make and they made the kitchen smell like grease. On those rare occasions when her mom made French fries, Kelly and her sister watched the pile of fries get doled out on the dinner plates. They scrutinized each stack to make sure one was not bigger than the other; and if one was, they fought to get the big one. Soon enough, her mother got sick of that, and she told them the way it was going to be.

M. Christine Stephens

The next time she made French fries, the oldest girl was going to get to divide them up, with one condition: the youngest girl was going to get to pick the stack she got first. Kelly told me that I would be amazed at the time it took for the stack to get divided, and how fairly proportioned they were. I love the French fry method; it was effective, and it put an end to the dilemma of who got more. I worked in health care a long, long time. I have been at people's deathbeds: sometimes, it brought out the very best in families; sometimes, it brought out the very worst. Before that loved one passed away, someone was mad. Someone accused someone of caring less, taking more, helping less, or worrying more about what they were going to get and less about what was fair to anyone else. I hope my kids never do that; it would break my heart. I want to think and believe that they would love each other, be fair and just, remember the good things I taught them, and be gracious and kind. Nothing would honor my memory more. Of all the jobs you ever do in life, you hope and pray you did that one right. You can be an employee, a coworker, a mother, a daughter, a sister, and a friend, and you always hope you do all of them right: but being a parent is the one job you hope more than all the others that you did right. It's not always true or right to say that everything your kids do is always your fault, because it's not. I saw a bumper sticker one time that said this: Don't take

On Life and Love

all of the credit or all of the blame for any choices your kids make, but I know what we say to them and do for them counts a lot; and in the end, despite whatever mistakes they make, we hope it yields sweet rewards.

Train up a child in the way he should go, and when he grows up he will not depart from it.

> Start children off on the way they should go,
> and even when they are old they will not turn
> from it. Proverbs 22:6

The Real Deal

I went to the police academy ten years ago. It was hard to find work in my profession at that time, so I applied, and was accepted, to the City of St. Petersburg to be a police officer. Now that I look back, I think it's not so much that I really wanted to be a police officer, but more that it was a secure city job with good benefits: and I had a son to raise and provide for on my own, and I could not find work in my physical therapy profession. I did great in the academy, passed the exams, qualified on the shooting and driving range, but deep down, I never really liked the work and was not cut out for it. They had a field training program, and one of the blocks of study was learning how to spot and detect counterfeit money. I was looking forward to going to that class. I thought the desk would be filled with every different kind of counterfeit money any crook ever thought of. I thought we would learn about all the different ways people made fake money, and what it all looked like. I thought we would have to study and remember all the subtle inaccuracies

On Life and Love

of the phony money floating around out there, but that's not how the class went. All there was on the instructor's desk was a twenty-dollar bill, and it was a real one, not a counterfeit. He told us we were going to start with a twenty-dollar bill, because that one was the one that was most often altered. I asked him where the counterfeit twenties were, but he told me he didn't bring any of those, and he wasn't going to. I asked him how we were going to learn what the fake ones looked like if we never see them, and he told me this, which was profound, and I never forgot it. He told me that he did not waste class time teaching people what was not real because counterfeiters will always change the way they do things. They will keep up with technology, and their methods of deception will always change, so it is pointless to try to learn them all. He told me that the best way to decipher whether or not something is false is to know for sure what is real. If you know the real thing, you will always spot the false one, no matter how many times it changes. People can make things tricky and confusing and confounding in a thousand different ways. It is deceptive; it looks real but it's not, and it will trick you every time. You will accept it as real and true, and you will do that not because it is, but because you don't fully and completely know what the real one looks like. Sure, we know at a quick glance what a twenty-dollar bill looks like, but we never really study every detail, every placement of every character, every component, the hue of color, and the thickness of that bill: and because we don't really know the real one inside and out, we are fooled by the fake, and we accept it. He told me that, always and forever, this rule is true: you will be far less likely to be fooled by the false things when you know the real ones.

My word is real.

> Then you will know the truth, and the truth will set you free. John 8:32

The Spider-Webbed Sewer Machine

My grandfather was not a bad man; in a thousand ways, he was a good man. My brother is a plumber, and he is a good man. He is hard-working and honest: he loves God, his wife and kids, and has built a successful plumbing business over the course of thirty-five plus years. Let's go back to my grandfather. Like I said, he was a good man in lots of ways; so I don't mean to give his reputation a black eye, but he was two things that I promised myself I would never be when I grew up: he was a pack rat and a miser. Before I start sounding too wicked here, let me say that I do remember the good things he did. He visited his grandkids, he took great care of my grandma through a long, lingering sickness until the day she died, he worked hard, and took care of his family. I don't ever want to be the person who remembers the bad in someone and doesn't acknowledge the good; that is unkind and unfair. There is good and bad in all of us, and I don't want people to remember only my faults and weaknesses, and never the good things I've done; but I have a lingering memory of him that sticks like glue. Why is it that we can do a hundred good things, but the bad one we do never really goes away? I hope someday, when I'm gone, people will remember the good things I've done and be merciful enough to blot out the bad, but I have to tell it so you will see that sometimes what we do in life leaves lasting legacies. Back to my brother, the plumber: when my brother was young and starting out in life, he had very little. We all had very little. He was one of seven kids, and although my father worked very hard to provide for us, there was never extra money to go around; so we learned young that if you want anything in life, you work hard to get it. That is a good life lesson, and we did not complain about it, then or now. My brother worked for a plumbing company, but wanted to venture out on his own. He figured he would be better off working for himself than someone else. My grandfather had an old sewer machine in his basement for years and years. He never used it; it was covered in spider webs, under a mound of junk behind another mound of junk. It was white with the fuzz of dust from decades in the basement. Back to my brother: sewer machines are expensive, but can yield a lot of money to a plumber, so he asked my grandfather to loan him the sewer machine; you know, the one behind the mound of junk with spider webs and white,

On Life and Love

fuzzy dust. My brother didn't ask him to give it, just loan it. The machine was useless to my grandfather, or at least it had been for many, many years. It would have been a tremendous help and a blessing to my brother. It would have helped my brother succeed, get up on his new business' wobbly legs, and make a go of a business in this hard, tough world. My grandfather told him no. I'm going to hold onto that machine because I might need it someday. When my grandfather died, and all the junk was removed from the basement, I watched that old sewer machine being carried up the basement steps, rusty now and outdated: old and useless and never used. My brother is much older now. He has lots of sewer machines. Maybe none of that matters anymore what happened a long time ago, but maybe it did, because it left a legacy. Sometimes you learn what to do in life by watching what your parents and grandparents did. Sometimes you learn from them what not to do. Here was an old man who had a chance to help a young and struggling grandson with a machine he had little to no use for. It would have cost him little or nothing to just say yes, sure you can borrow that sewer machine; in fact, it will be my gift to you. It can say I love you, good luck in your new business venture; I am proud of you and I wish you all the success in the world. There are no pockets in funeral clothes. There doesn't need to be, because there is nothing you can take with you. I

M. Christine Stephens

have never seen a hearse pulling a trailer full of things. Things come and go: houses, cars, jobs, and money come and go. Sewer machines come and go. It's never about what we have, but who we can bless and help with what we have. In the end, that's all that will ever matter, and the legacy we will leave behind. I think about that every time I am at my brother's plumbing shop and I see a sewer machine. I don't mean to, but I can't help it. My mind just goes there. Was holding onto that machine worth it in the end? I ask God to help me remember that. Remember to be generous, to give someone a leg up. Money is just a tool, so are things. The intention should be not to hoard either, but to use it to bless, help, lift up, and say I love you. If your money and your possessions are not doing that, you are wasting them. How much better a legacy it would have been if every time we see sewer machines, we could say, remember when you were just starting out, and Grandpa gave you that sewer machine?

The Lord loves a cheerful giver.

> Each of you should give what you have decided in your heart to give, not reluctantly or under compulsion, for God loves a cheerful giver.
> II Corinthians 9:7

They Are All Hypocrites

My friend told me she used to have to go to church every Sunday. Her parents made her go, and when she got old enough to leave home, she never went again. They are all hypocrites in church, she told me, and that is why she would not go. She told me the pastor at the last church she went to left his wife for a younger lady there, and the pastor before him just begged for money all the time. She told me she thought people went to church to see who else went to get something from God, to do their duties, to show off a car or a dress, or brag about a new house, or to make other people think they were good. Maybe some of that was true some of the time, but really, we are all hypocrites some of the time. A hypocrite is anyone who says or does something they know they should not say or do, and that is pretty much all of us at one time or another. God can still work through people that don't do everything right. He has to, or else who would He have because we are all that way sometimes. No one has to be perfect for God to use them. No one is perfect;

so if God waited for the perfect person to reach out, He would never find one. The people in church will never be perfect; neither will you. Cut everyone a break. Stop looking around at who does what wrong. Don't let that rattle you. When Jesus was here on earth, and He picked people to follow Him, serve Him, and be His friend, He did not do a criminal background check first. He did not judge them or wait for them to be good enough or right enough or perfect enough. He knew that wasn't happening. He just loved them and let them do what good they could do anyway. With all their flaws and mistakes and weaknesses, He let them know Him, love Him, serve Him, teach His word, and be His friend. He used prostitutes, murderers, liars, and thieves. He knew they would sometimes fail. He knew they wouldn't always say and do the right things. He knew they would not always honor Him, but He took them in; He let them serve Him, and He let them tell other people about Him. Don't worry so much about who does what in church. It's not our jobs to judge them. The same judgement stick we use to judge other people will be used against us some day.

Judge not lest you be judged.

> Do not judge or you too will be judged.
>
> Matthew 7:1

Changing Grace

My friend had a son that was caught up in the misery of drug addiction. This friend was a kind and devoted mother. She put her kid's needs before her own, taught them about God, worked hard, kept their home clean, did not drink or party, or drop them off to be cared for by anyone else while she went out to have fun. Her son went to a fundamental school, Sunday school, youth group, played little league football and softball. She helped him with his homework every night, read to him before bed, kept him clean and well fed, loved, cared for and protected, and, by every standard you could measure, she was a good mother. How could this have happened? If you would have told her this would happen years ago, she would never in a million years believe you. Kids like hers do not become drug addicts. That happens to other kids: kids from horrible families, kids who no one cares about, kids who have no direction in life, but not my kid. Why would this, or how could this, ever happen to my son? She told me that she used to be extremely hard and critical about parents that let their kids grow up to be drug users. What kind of garbage parents must they be to have ever let anything like this happen? How could they have so miserably failed to do the single most important job God ever gave them to do on this earth? How could they have produced a drug addict, who then becomes a liar and a thief, who does not work, has no ambition or motivation, and who lives every day of his life only to find drugs? She told me that the pain of this had become unbearable. She told me that never a day in her life had she used drugs. Where could he ever have gotten that example, because it surely was not from her. She told me that every day she was heartsick, embarrassed, worried, and ashamed. She told me that the sun never shines one single day in her world. She said she cries when she does anything; she cries at red lights and at work. She does not want to talk to friends, and she doesn't know who to talk to. "It just hurts all the time. It hurts so much that I can feel a physical pain. Nothing takes it away. There is no escape from this, not even sleep. My gut is tight, and I am afraid every time the phone rings that something terrible has happened to him, or that he has caused something terrible to happen to someone else. If I have to live in this world this way, I don't want to be here. I would escape and end this, but he needs me, and then I would not be here to help him. What do you say to someone in that kind

On Life and Love

of grief? She told me about Christmas Eve for her, not long ago. She was having family for dinner. She shopped for ham and all the trimmings. She got to the register and swiped her debit card; it was declined. She told the clerk that was not possible; that her paycheck was electronically deposited every Friday, and she just got paid. There is money in this account. She swiped it again, and, again, it was declined. How embarrassing. She told the clerk there had to be some mistake. Her sister was with her and paid the bill for her. She vowed to be at the bank in the morning and find out what happened. Next day, she called the bank and checked her balance. Sure enough, the money was gone; withdrawn with her debit card two days ago. She told them she did not know how that could happen, and she did not withdraw that money. She demanded an investigation, demanded that the video at the ATM machine be viewed, and the thief be caught. She was told just this: We will take the time and steps to pull that video. We will investigate, and we will find out who used your card, but before we do, we are going to ask you this. Could anyone in your family have done this? Anyone who knows your PIN number? Here is how this works. You ask your family first. Once we pull the video, we will prosecute whoever did this, whether you agree to it or not. We will have them arrested and charged, just so you know. Now, would you like us to do that? She was stunned, and did not want to let herself even think what she was beginning to think. Could my son have done this? No, he would never ever do that to me. No, she told them, please don't. Thank you anyway. The trouble grew deeper. He was arrested, incarcerated, and now he had a felony and a criminal record. She made the sickening treks to jail to visit. She wrote him every day. She cried all the time. This young life was destroyed; a precious only son. She was a nurse, and she went through her day and delivered care, worked hard, paid bills, and cleaned the house. She went through the motions, but she didn't live. She struggled to eat and to breath and to sleep and to live. She went into patients' rooms and saw pictures of their sons on their tabletops: pictures of their sons in Navy uniforms, pictures of them in college caps and gowns, pictures of them in police uniforms. Her son wore inmate numbers. She remembered a scene from an old movie she saw. A drug addict son pulls a gun on his mother and demands her wallet. She had given him money a hundred times before: before she understood how not to enable; before when she thought it would help him; before when she felt sorry for him; and before when she wanted to be there for him. Now she knew that to hand him money may be to kill him. It could be what purchases the last lethal dose. Shoot me, she told him. There could be no pain that equals what I live with now. It would bring an end to this horrible

On Life and Love

thing. Every family with a drug-addicted child could write the same story. The names and faces and details may change, but the story is always the same. They never get an answer when they ask why. They say all the things any parent would say to try and change this dark, sad thing, but it is like talking to a wall. There seems to be no soul inside that body, no mind that connects or hears. The lights are out, and there is no one home in the heart of that lost and damaged, precious child. The stronghold of addiction is demonic. Who can fight against it? They steal and lie, they use and abuse, they neglect themselves and their children, and they bring unbelievable sadness and shame to themselves and their families. The devil is a cruel master to serve. No one can change them, no one but God, and only God. He can and He will, He does and He did, and how do we ever thank Him? There is nowhere God's spirit cannot go. It penetrates prison walls and the darkness of addiction. He heals, restores, and delivers. He answers prayer, and He sets the captive free.

I know the plans I have for you. They are for good and not evil. They are to prosper you, to give you a future and a hope.

> "For I know the plans I have for you", declares the Lord. "plans to prosper you and not to harm you, plans to give you hope and a future."
> Jeremiah 29:11

Miss June and the Norfolk Pine Tree

I worked in a nursing home in St. Pete; that's where I met Miss June. Miss June was eighty-two years old and sharp as a tack. Sometimes I would stick my head in her room just to say hello. Nobody ever came to visit Miss June much; I didn't visit as much as I should because I was so busy there. One afternoon I went in to say hello. Miss June was asleep on her bed with a tiny Norfolk pine tree in her hand; it was the kind you buy at Christmas time, a few inches tall wrapped with shiny red paper at the bottom. It was a little living tree, and it could be replanted in the ground or in another pot. Miss June was asleep, but her hands were wrapped around the bottom of this little pine tree. Dirt was scattered on the bedspread and sheets. I took the little pine tree out of her hands and set it on her windowsill. I tried not to wake her up, but she woke up anyway. Miss June, I told her, you fell asleep with your pine tree in your hands, and now the dirt is everywhere. What made you want to hold your pine tree?

On Life and Love

There is a shaft of sunlight she said, that comes into this room every day about this time. This little pine tree needs that sunlight or it will die. It has to stay alive until this weekend. I have property that has been in my family for a long, long time. My son died when he was just a little boy, and he is buried very near there. This pine tree is for him. We will plant it by his grave so it can grow and live there. My family is coming to take me there on Saturday. This pine tree needs the sunlight to stay strong until then. I have seen hundreds of patients, maybe even thousands, and mostly it is always just sad. Nobody much comes to visit. Pretty much they are alone, even the ones with family. Kids grow up: they are busy with jobs, responsibilities, and kids of their own. It's not that they don't love their aging parents, or maybe it is that sometimes they do and sometimes they don't; but either way, they don't visit much. Miss June kind of got forgotten about: forgotten in the busyness of life, the shuffle of duties that her adult children had, the hardship of earning a living and raising children and running households, and the craziness that is America today. So Miss June lays in her bed and holds a baby pine tree that will honor a life she loved a long time ago. I went through my work day there every day, and I hate to think that I became callous or insensitive, but maybe I did. There was just a tremendous amount of loneliness in that place, and if you took it all to heart all day every day, it would become overwhelming; but on that day and in that room, a sadness came over me that I could not ignore. Maybe Miss June wondered why they don't visit. Maybe she thought that this son would have come if he could have. Maybe she knew the time she had with him here on this earth was all too short; but whatever she thought, this tree was for him and if she had to hold it in a single ray of sun to keep it alive, then she would. At work the next day, I told a Filipino coworker all about Miss June and the little pine tree. I asked her what nursing homes in the Philippines were like, but she seemed a little confused. I don't know, she said. We don't have too many there. Well, who takes care of the elderly?" I asked. She said, "We do." Families take care of each other there. Our aging parents and grandparents live with us. Seems like here in America, people are busier. They earn a lot, and they have more than we do. It's just different here, I guess. Her responses were not meant to be critical or judgmental towards us; I think it was just an observation. People come and go more often in America; sometimes even family comes and goes, or at least comes less often. It made me sad for every Miss June. Some of them are bitter because they feel forgotten. Some make excuses for their adult kids, telling me how busy they are, how successful they have become, how well they live: the houses and cars they can afford, and the American Dream they have achieved. Miss June

On Life and Love

did not seem bitter or angry, just determined to hold a pine tree in a ray of sunlight that would let it live so it could grow where she thought it belonged. Maybe she came to a place of peace that some of us never get to, or to a knowledge that escapes some.

I will never leave you or forsake you. I am the friend that sticks closer than a brother. I am with you always.

> Be strong and courageous. Do not be afraid or terrified because of them, for the Lord your God goes with you: He will never leave you or forsake you. Deuteronomy 31:6

Mr. Garwood and Woody

When I was eighteen years old, I worked in an animal hospital. I just left home; I was young and poor, and I didn't have any direction in life. On the weekdays, I worked at the front desk. I answered the phones and signed the animals in, but on the weekends, for extra money, I worked in the kennel. I fed the border animals and the surgery animals. I took them for walks, I cleaned their cages, and whatever else needed done. One day, an old man named Mr. Garwood came into the animal hospital. He asked me if we board dogs, and I told him yes we did. He asked me if we would board his old dog Woody. He told me that Woody was all he really had in the world. He told me that Woody and him have been together for seventeen years. He told me he found Woody in a dumpster on Christmas Eve seventeen years ago. He said this to me, I am old and I have no one. I have no children, and my family is gone, and that is why I named him after me. Woody is all I have, so you better take care of him right. I am going in for surgery tomorrow. I need someone

On Life and Love

to take care of Woody. I assured him we would take good care of his dog. Bring him in when you're ready, and we will take care of him right. The next morning, Mr. Garwood came with Woody. He brought an old, brown grocery bag filled with Woody's things. There was a blanket so Woody would not feel the cold of the kennel floor. He needs this blanket, said Mr. Garwood. He is old, too, just like me. He has arthritis, too, just like I do. We don't like cold, Woody and me, so make sure he gets his blanket. Mr. Garwood stated that he wrote a note for Woody's care: when to feed him, how to feed him, what to do and not to do, and I better do it just the way he wrote it. I promised I would. There were dog toys in there, too. Lots of dog toys and Alpo®; more Alpo® than I figured any dog would ever eat, even though I told him we have dog food here, but I was warned that Woody would not eat anything else. Then there was applesauce, lots and lots of applesauce. He made sure he told me how much Woody loved applesauce, and that I was not to forget to give it to him. I promised I would. So I took Woody back to the kennel as soon as Mr. Garwood would let him go. I thought about how sad that must be, to face surgery and no one cared but Woody. I was too busy to think about it for too long. I checked Woody in; others were lined up behind him, so I couldn't dwell on sadness very long. Good luck, I told him, because it was my job to be kind and friendly, even to nasty old Mr. Garwood. If anyone made it hard to be friendly, it was Mr. Garwood. He sat there with Woody as long as he could, until finally a taxi came for the old man, and he was gone. I put Woody in the kennel run, laid his blanket down, closed the door, and went back to work. Later that day, I went back to check on Woody. I emptied the dog toys from his bag into his run, and it was then that I read the note. The instructions were rigid, numbered, stern, direct, and very clear. Applesauce at nine am, only after one can of Alpo®, and not before. When you walk him, do it slow (underlined three times in thick, black Magic Marker®). Remember I told you he has arthritis, so don't walk fast. One can of applesauce at noon, and a can of Alpo® at six pm. Don't forget the applesauce, because Woody loves it (again, underlined three times with that fat, black, menacing Magic Marker®). If any note could say "I mean business", it was that one. No one was going to do Woody wrong, and no one was going to not do things the way Woody liked them. I got the message, so every day, I did things for Woody just that way. That was Monday, and every day that followed, I did it to Woody's liking. Now Woody was the kind of dog that inhaled his food. He didn't nibble or take his time; he sucked food down with a vengeance. Woody loved to chow. Saturday came, and I was always the weekend kennel help. I punched in at nine am, like I always did. I cleaned the cages,

On Life and Love

fed the cats, changed the litter, and started on the dogs. One can of Alpo® for Woody. I braced the door of his run, because when food was coming, Woody couldn't wait. Today, though, was different. Woody wouldn't eat today. Instead of lunging for the bowl, Woody howled. He put his head way back and howled a long, lonely howl, just like a wolf does. I just left the food and figured he would eat it later. I took care of all the animals, finished up, and went home. Monday morning, I was back to work at the reception desk when the call came from a social worker at St. Anthony's Hospital. "Is this Northeast Animal Hospital?" she asked. Yep, I told her it was. She asked me if we had a boarder dog for a man named Mr. Garwood. I told her we did. She told me that Mr. Garwood passed away this past Saturday morning. She kept talking, but I really didn't hear her much. It was chilling to hear that Mr. Garwood was dead. My thoughts went back to Saturday morning; I know now what I didn't figure out then. I know, I told her. How would you know that, she asked. I just told her, Woody told me. I was sad and sorry. Sorry I wasn't kinder, sorry I was too busy to try to understand him, and sorry I let the crotchety, old guy get to me. I could have engaged Mr. Garwood more. I could have talked to him longer about Woody, seeing how that was probably his favorite topic, but I didn't because he was curt and bossy and rude. I will do it different next time.

M. Christine Stephens

Be ye kind in all things.

> Be kind and compassionate to one another, forgiving each other, just as in kjChrist god forgave you. Ephesians 4:32

Saltwater Fish

I love to look at saltwater fish: the brilliant colors, the shapes and sizes, the details of the stripes, yellow fins on blue fish, seahorses, starfish, sharks, skates, and rays. Who, but a divine and masterful creator, could make a saltwater fish? Actually, you could say this about a million things: your baby's face, the human eye, a mountain, a sunset, the moon, stars, sun, and sea fall into that category, too; and I know that, but it just seemed like during the lowest times in my life, always and what seemed like coincidentally, I would be somewhere that I would see a saltwater fish. Once it was at a pet shop, once it was at Tampa Aquarium, and once it was in my living room watching a Natural Geographic film. During some of the saddest and scariest times in life, during the times I have wondered where could God be in all of this, I would see a saltwater fish. You know God is real, and He cares about us. You know He is there, but you don't yet see the evidence of Him in what you are going through. You wonder why He let this happen, and what you are going to do about it. You wonder if everything you learned about God is real and true. You wonder about the millions of people on this earth; can He really know and love all of them? Does He really guide and lead us? Does He really look down from heaven and have His eye on the sparrow? Does He get personally involved in my issues, this vast and great Creator of all heaven and earth, and saltwater fish? Why doesn't He just talk to us, in a voice we can hear? Why doesn't He just knock on the door and come in our living room, or meet us at a park bench? Why doesn't He let us know that He is really real, really there, really concerned and involved and has it handled? Then, I realized that He does. He shows us in a million ways, but for me, He has a favorite way. He shows me saltwater fish.

> Be still and know that I am God.
> He says, "Be still and know that I am God; I will be exalted among the nations, I will be exalted in all the earth." Psalms 46:10

Final Payment for Kaitlin

All through high school and middle school, my daughter was best friends with a girl named Kaitlin. I had Kaitlin almost all the time. She stayed overnight for weeks at a time. She had an absentee father that she rarely saw or spoke to. Her mother divorced him a long time ago, and he lived far away and really just seemed to have better things to do then bother with Kaitlin. Her mother was there, but struggled with depression, couldn't hold down a job for very long, didn't have much energy to invest in Kaitlin, and was happy when she was with us because it was less for her to think about and do. She was an only child, the result of a brief dating relationship between her mom and the man you couldn't really call a father, who lived somewhere in Las Vegas. I loved Kaitlin. Something about her personality was unique. She did not let the grim circumstances of her situation get to her. She excelled in school and she laughed a lot, worked hard at an after-school job, got excellent grades, and was a joy to be around. You knew not to

M. Christine Stephens

expect much from Kaitlin's mom: as far as giving the girls a ride, offering to "take them if you'll pick them up"; never sent her to the house with a dime, so any movie, lunch-out or anything I did with the girls was on me or it wasn't going to happen. I did it for Kaitlin as much as for my own daughter, because the two were inseparable best friends. Kaitlin went on family vacations with us. I had her for Christmas and Thanksgiving, and bought her dress for their high school homecoming. I just kind of adopted her without the paperwork, if you know what I mean. She introduced me to Nirvana and Green Day music, stuff I would have never listened to if she hadn't brought it into the house. She dyed her hair green, worn safety pins in her pierced ears instead of earrings, and did things that "pushed the envelope" of conventional behavior, at least for back then, and seemed to scream, "Will somebody please notice me?" She never seemed to feel sorry for herself: it just seemed like she expected her father to be distant and uninvolved; expected her mother to be disconnected because that's the was it always was for Kaitlin, and she never knew it to be any other way. Throughout the years of middle school and high school, Kaitlin was an almost permanent figure my home, a member of the family; a plate was almost always set for Kaitlin at dinner time because she was almost always there. Humor was her coping mechanism. She was quick with a joke, always laughing, and able to see humor in the most ordinary things, so she really was a lot of fun to have around. She told me that her father did send a child support check that her mother had to fight for more than once, took him to court, waited for the check to come that was always late, took him back to court two or three more times when he tried to duck out of his responsibility, and had to "wrestle with him like an alligator" to get it. Kaitlin's father resented having to support her, and she knew it; yet I had never seen her sad or depressed. She was always high gear, top speed, full of fun, and ready for whatever was next. She reminded me of a tough and resilient plant. I love to garden, so I have to make this analogy. I have purchased some plants that, no matter what I did, they did not thrive. I kept them in the proper amount of sun. I gave them the richest soil, I fertilized and watered with not too much and not too little amount. I did everything just the way I was supposed to, but no matter what I did, they died; and I'm a pretty good gardener. I've purchased other plants that were like Kaitlin. They were tough and strong and resilient. No matter what you did or failed to do, they not only lived, but seemed to flourish. It didn't matter if you forgot about them, neglected them, if you failed to water or fertilize or plant correctly, they still grew tall and strong. They are a gardener's dream, just like Kaitlin seemed to be a parent's dream. She seemed to thrive on neglect. Everyone in her life who should have loved her, cherished her, invested in her, and become proud of her wasn't. The two people in her world that should have encouraged her, taught her, guided her, and protected her didn't. Still, she thrived, or so it seemed. She was motivated, smart, driven, warm, friendly, outgoing, funny, and fun. She was upbeat, respectful, courteous, and grateful for everything you did for her. The grime that was all around her at home never seemed to stick to her, except for once. She came Friday after school to the house, like she always did. Her face was swollen, her eyes were red, and everything in her demeanor was different. Something was terribly wrong in Kaitlin's world; a world that seemed to be untouchable by the things that were wrong in her life, and to a kid that seemed to master the art of being impervious to rejection. I knew that whatever it was that she was grieving about that day was heavier than any child should have to carry. She went into my daughter's bedroom and sobbed. It was the racking kind of sob that leaves you sucking for the next breath. I knocked on the door and asked her if I could help. I asked her to tell me what happened, if she felt she could. I wanted to be there to comfort her, just like I would have if she were my own. No matter what I said or offered to do, it didn't help. Finally, she told me this. She told me she saw a check on her kitchen counter at home. It was from her deadbeat

On Life and Love

dad somewhere out there in Las Vegas. It was a child support check written to her mother for her, and although the rest of the check was written with a blue ink pen, the memo section of the check was filled out in thick, black Magic Marker®, and underlined twice. It read FINAL CHECK FOR KAITLIN. That man said a thousand words in those four. He said I don't want you, I never wanted you, I resented paying for you, and I am glad I am finished. He said you are eighteen now, and I am no longer legally forced to take care of you, or even think about you. Those four words said good bye, good riddance, and don't ever ask for or expect anything from me ever again. Words are powerful, and with just a few, you can say a lot. They can reveal what is truly on our minds, in our heads, and in our hearts. They can lift up or tear down, they can heal or wound, they can love or hate, and they can build or demolish. They can tell anyone who hears them "This is what I really think".

Out of the heart, the mouth speaks.

> But the things that come out of a person's mouth come from the heart and these defile them. Matthew 15:18

The Spirit Realm

There is a world all around us, but we only see part of it. We only see the part we can see with our eyes, feel with our hands, and hear with our ears. There is another world all around us, too, but it's a different realm. We can't see it, touch it, taste it or hear it, but it is real. Before you think I'm crazy, spooky, paranormal or over the edge, let me try to explain. Have you ever been in a room, maybe reading or typing or occupied in any way, and someone comes in that room behind you? You can't see him/her, and you didn't hear him/her come in, but you can feel the presence of someone in the room. Here's another example: have you ever spoken to someone you have never met before, someone you don't know, and you sense that something about that person is either very right, or very wrong, or very confused or angry, or upbeat or curious or whatever the list of a hundred things could be? A lot of times it's not anything they said or did; it's just a feeling you get when you're around them. It's a sense, a vibe; call it what you want, but it's something and you pick up

On Life and Love

on it. It's hard to explain and figure out, and you couldn't really define it if you had to; it's just there. It's kind of like the times people say, "Something told me not to do that," or "There was just something about him I liked" or "I just had a feeling about that." Or "I'm not too sure, but I think there is something fishy about that." You know what I mean. I'm sure it has happened to you. The spirit world is real: good spirits, bad spirits, but they are real and they are out there, thick as molasses but invisible to the eye. We live in both a physical realm and a spiritual realm; there is no denying that.

Dear friends, do not believe every spirit, but test the spirits to see whether or not they are from God.

> Dear friends, do not believe every spirit, but test the spirits to see whether they are from God, because many false prophets have gone out into the world. I John 4:1

The Jigsaw Puzzle

When I was a kid, I loved doing jigsaw puzzles. I would study the picture on the box, and keep the box right beside me as I assembled the pieces. The corner pieces went in a separate pile. The light colors, dark colors, the pieces that would become water or trees or sky or grass all went in their own separate piles. I had a method and a plan to put together jigsaw puzzles. I was good at it, fast and efficient, and no one had a better method then I did. One time, though, my grandmother made me do one without ever looking at the picture on the box first. Now I have to tell you about the yard sale house. These two things seem unrelated, but I will tie them together soon, so bear with me. One day, my brother and I went to a yard sale. We just liked looking through the junk, and hoping we found something that we thought was a treasure. We were out in the country, and we stopped at this old mobile home when we saw the sign in the yard that said YARD SALE. We dug through old pots and pans, car parts, old clothes and shoes, books, coffee

On Life and Love

mugs, and blankets with threads hanging off them. You know what I'm talking about; you've seen all that junk at yard sales, too. The little old lady of the house, and yard sale shopkeeper, seemed eager just to chat. She seemed kind of lonely, you know the kind of folks I'm talking about. They are hungry to converse, or more accurately, hungry for someone to listen to them, so we engaged her in conversation about old Coke® bottles, lamps and end tables, and she just spoke up, out of the blue, and said this to me, "Do you see my mobile home behind me? My husband and I are getting a new one, a smaller one that is less to cool, heat and clean. We don't want this one anymore, but we don't want to pay the money to have it removed from our property, so if you will pay that, you can have it. Who charges fifty cents at a yard sale for a coffee mug, but gives away a house? Do you mind if I look inside, I asked. She told me I could, but not to expect much. She told me they raised six kids in there, never kept up on much of anything in there because life just seemed busy and hard enough. I was only inside for a minute when I saw exactly what she meant, and she was right. The carpets were filthy and stained with dog pee everywhere. The stove and frig were that ugly avocado color of yesteryear, splattered with rust. Every countertop and cupboard was stained, chipped, burned with a hot pan, or a cigarette from who knows when. The tubs, toilets, and sinks were plastic, and either cracked, bent, or out of order. The old vinyl on the floor was peeled back and nasty, the faucets leaked, and the air conditioner broke a long time ago. The light fixtures were cracked or non-existent. Who would ever in a million years live like this, or tackle this home repair nightmare? It didn't need TLC, it needed to be put out of its misery. Wow. Sometimes, we are very careful to not let the look on our faces reveal what we are thinking. This was one of those times. I smiled politely as she showed me around, from room to room, as she apologized for the place, explaining that the kids were a handful, and they were hard on everything. She said her boys loved cats and dogs and had dozens, and were never very good at cleaning up after them, and she just couldn't keep up. I could tell she was embarrassed about everything, but desperate to get this old mobile home off of her property to make space for a new one, and she was hoping to do it for free. I asked her if I could give it some thought and thanked her for the offer. I stepped outside with my brother so that I could be out of there and breath air that was not polluted with the stench of cat urine, cooking grease, and cigarettes. When my brother and I were out the door, I told him that whoever would take her up on her offer was crazy, and I thought he would agree, but he didn't. He told me, "You're not crazy if you do; you're crazy if you don't. Take this house. Pay someone to cut it

On Life and Love

in half, drag it off of her property and onto yours, and just gut it out. Rip out every tub, toilet, sink, appliance, cabinet, and countertop. Tear out the rugs, rip up the vinyl, just take it down to the walls, and then, little by little, and as you can afford it, re-do it inch by inch. Work a few months and buy new toilets. Save for a year and pay a kitchen guy to remodel. Work six months, and buy a scratch-and-dent stove and frig, do some cosmetic stuff, and put some cheap laminate on the floor. It will take some time and money, and a lot of 'sweat equity', but in the end you can make it cute, clean, and sweet, and you won't have a mortgage. It sounded just crazy enough to work, so I took her up on her offer, and did exactly what my brother suggested. It took about two years and a ton of work, but when it was done, it was cuter than Christmas. I did the walls in knotty pine tongue and groove all over, new everything everywhere. I did it little by little, and as I could afford it and pay for it with cash as I went along. I hung decorations like Cracker Barrel, befitting of a country house in the woods, and I loved it. I sold my two-story townhouse in the city: the one with a fat mortgage and a homeowner's association fee tacked on; the one I didn't need anymore to house two kids who were grown and gone and on their own. I didn't know it then, but God was setting me up for a greater thing, another time in life down the road a way, but a time when I would need to have a house that was paid in full and mortgage-free: a time when I could rest, work less, and write this book. You see, it was like the jigsaw puzzle, the one Grandma made us do where you had to finish the puzzle without ever looking at the picture on the box. You don't know what it's going to look like. You don't know what it's supposed to look like. You stumble through it; sometimes it's frustrating, sometimes it's maddening, and sometimes you don't know why you're even doing it. Sometimes, you don't want to finish it. Sometimes, God gives us gifts that are all put together already, like our health, our kids, our ability to work, and a thousand other things. Sometimes He gives us things we can't yet see. He sees them, but we don't see them yet. They will help us down the road and become a greater gift than we would have ever imagined, kind of like putting together a jigsaw puzzle before you're ever allowed to see the picture on the box.

> Taste and see that the Lord is good; blessed is the man who takes refuge in Him. Psalms 34:8

CPSIA information can be obtained
at www.ICGtesting.com
Printed in the USA
LVHW01s1215131117
556086LV00004B/316/P